THESE ARE OUR BODIES

FOR INTERMEDIATE

Church Publishing
NEW YORK

PARTICIPANT BOOK

Scripture quotations from the CEB used with permission. All rights reserved. Common English Bible, Copyright 2011.

Scripture from the *New Revised Standard Version Bible (NRSV)* © 1989 by the Division of Christian Education of the National Council of Churches of Christ in the USA. Used by permission.

A catalog record of this book is available from the Library of Congress.

Church Publishing Incorporated
19 East 34th Street
New York, NY 10016

Cover design by: Jennifer Kopec, 2 Pug Design
Typeset by: Progressive Publishing Services

ISBN-13: 978-0-89869-019-4 (pbk.)

Printed in the United States of America

CONTENTS

INTRODUCTION

Welcome to *These Are Our Bodies*!

You are about to begin a journey of learning and discovery. You might have lots of questions and wonders. We hope that you will make connections between your faith and your growing body. Your parent(s) are participants in this program, too. They also want to be part of your journey.

To help you along this expedition, this is your *Participant Book*. We will actually be calling you a tween . . . you are not a young child anymore (you know that) and not quite a teenager, yet. So you are a tween.

This book is for you. It is a place for you to journal, write, and doodle. We hope that you will take time to reflect along the way and that you will have fun, too.

Jenny Beaumont and Abbi Long

WE ARE WONDERFULLY MADE

"For it was you who formed my inward parts;
you knit me together in my mother's womb.
I praise you, for I am fearfully and
wonderfully made.
Wonderful are your works; that I know
very well."
—Psalm 139:13–14

HOLY COVENANT

H stands for Honesty.

O stands for Openness.

L stands for Learning Together.

Y stands for Your Questions.

Write down any concerns or worries you have about this program.

What are you wondering about? What are you looking forward to?

YOU ARE WONDERFULLY MADE

"For it was you who formed my inward parts; you knit me
together in my mother's womb. I praise you, for I am
fearfully and wonderfully made.
Wonderful are your works; that I know very well."
—Psalm 139:13–14

When the passage says, "For it was you," who is the "you?"

What do you think "inward parts" are? Give an example if you can.

What do you think the passage means when it says, "knit?" Does it mean like a person making a scarf out of yarn? How should we understand that verb?

Think about the word "wonderfully." To make it easier, let's just use "wonderful" for now. What are some synonyms, or other words that mean about the same thing?

Here are some ideas[1] . . . can you find them in this word search?

amazing

astonishing

awesome

brilliant

cool

excellent

fabulous

fantastic

incredible

magnificent

marvelous

outstanding

phenomenal

remarkable

surprising

terrific

tremendous

```
P  B  T  P  G  C  M  Y  E  I  P  T  X  G  I
R  H  N  N  X  N  F  A  C  M  E  X  E  R  G
E  F  E  W  A  C  I  G  R  R  O  U  W  N  L
M  A  L  N  L  I  O  H  R  V  S  S  I  Y  O
A  B  L  T  O  I  L  I  S  U  E  D  E  I  O
R  U  E  N  B  M  F  L  R  I  N  L  B  W  C
K  L  C  E  E  I  E  P  I  A  N  P  O  J  A
A  O  X  C  C  I  R  N  T  R  J  O  K  U  W
B  U  E  I  D  I  D  S  A  N  B  N  T  O  S
L  S  B  F  S  N  T  O  Q  L  N  N  Q  S  F
E  K  D  I  S  U  O  D  N  E  M  E  R  T  A
E  A  N  N  O  I  N  C  R  E  D  I  B  L  E
E  G  L  G  F  A  N  T  A  S  T  I  C  T  Y
V  P  E  A  G  N  I  Z  A  M  A  J  Q  F  L
E  P  O  M  C  O  O  J  T  M  I  N  Z  A  G
```

....

When you hear these words, how do they make you feel?

Draw an emoji or face to help demonstrate your feelings. You can draw more than one.

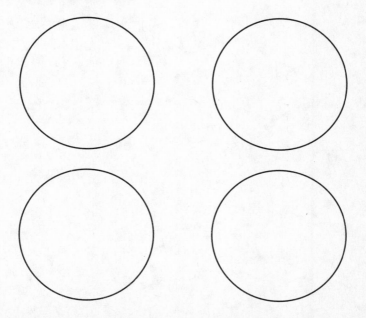

What questions do you have?

Fill in the blanks. Add more if you want.

I wonder

I also wonder

SCRIPTURE STUDY

This is for you to do on your own when you want. We will use Psalm 139:1–23 for our closing prayer.

- Read the passage again.

- Circle the word "God" every place you see it.

- Draw a heart around the word "I" every place you see it.

- Box in any action words or verbs.

- Illustrate the action words or verbs. You could draw stick people or faces or other sketches. You can draw them below or in the margins next to the verses in the Psalm that follows.

PSALM 139:1 - 23

God, you know me better than anyone, even myself.
You know what I'm doing, you even know what I'm
thinking.
When I move around or when I lay down, when I walk
or sit still, you always know where I am.
There's nothing I say that you haven't already figured
I'm going to say.
God, you know me inside and out.

You are in front of me to guide me, behind me to
protect me, and I feel your hand on my shoulder, so I
know I'm not alone. That's almost too good to be true.
God, you know me inside and out.

Is there anywhere I can go where you are NOT?
Not any place that I know. Can I run fast enough to
get away from your Spirit?
God, you know me inside and out.

You yourself created all my parts. You pieced me together in my mother's womb. You did an excellent job making me, and I thank you for that. You are amazing. That's for sure.
God, you know me inside and out.

You are in front of me to guide me, behind me to protect me, and I feel your hand on my shoulder, so I know I'm not alone.
It's almost too good to be true.
God, you know me inside and out.

You've known me forever. Your eyes could see my arms and legs, even before they were fully formed. Day by day I grew bigger until I was finally me with all my parts, ready to be born.
God, you know me inside and out.

I'm amazed by your deep thoughts, O God; the number of them astounds me. I couldn't possibly count them all, because there are more of them than grains of sand on the shore. If I were to count them it would take forever, and by then I'd be as old as you. *God, you know me inside and out.*

If I soar into the sky, you're there. If I lay down in the dirt, you are there too. If I fly like a bird to the middle of the biggest ocean, and then dive down into the waters, I wouldn't be surprised that you're there, too, to guide me.
God, you know me inside and out.

If I say, oh my God, I feel like it's the darkest night
even in the middle of the day, I'm so sad . . . you tell
me, it's alright. Dark or day, I am with you.
Figure out who I am, God. Then let me know.
Look into my deepest thoughts. I'm glad to have you
here with me, to help me and lead me back to you.
God, you know me inside and out.[2]

----

2   Lyn Zill Briggs, *God's Word, My Voice: A Lectionary for Children* (New York: Church Publishing, 2016), 233, 156. Used with permission.

SESSION 2

WE ARE
UNIQUE

Yet, O Lord, you are our Father;
we are the clay, and you are our potter;
we are all the work of your hand.
—Isaiah 64:8

Dear God, help me to live each day knowing that I am created by you. Your hand has made me and holds me tight. You are like a potter and I am like clay. Thank you for all you have done for me. Help me to remember that you are my potter not only in what I say, but in what I do as well. All praise be to you, O God. *Amen*.

Our prayer was about God being like a potter and molding us.
In the book of Isaiah, we read:

> Yet, O Lord, you are our Father;
> we are the clay, and you are our potter;
> we are all the work of your hand.
> —Isaiah 64:8

What does it mean to be the work of God's hands?

What do we make with our hands?

When we think of being God's handy work, sometimes we think about God being strong, sure, and gentle. Write down some examples of someone being both strong and gentle. Draw a picture if you prefer.

Sometimes, we can forget that we are wonderfully made and that we are God's handiwork.

BODY PRESSURE

What are some of the pressures around our bodies?

What are some expectations that you feel about your body?

How would it feel to grow up to be an everyday hero?

God has created you to do very special things. You are created good, and perfect just the way you are. Sometimes when we begin to grow up, we become self-conscious about the way we look and compare ourselves to others.

AFFIRMATION STATEMENTS

If God were to whisper encouragement to you, want would that encouragement be?

Each of us hears God's voice in a different way. This affirmation message can be an important part of growing. The messages that we tell ourselves mold and shape us. This message about you and God's love for you will help you to know that you are uniquely created.

What message might God say about you, about you growing up, or about your body? Write it here:

Thank you God for creating me perfectly and uniquely! You are an awesome Creator. Thank you for making me the work of your hand. Sometimes I forget how cool it is to be your child. *Amen*.

SESSION 3

WE ARE
A MIRACLE

. . . the Lord God formed the human from the topsoil
of the fertile land and blew life's breath into his
nostrils. The human came to life.
—Genesis 2:7 (CEB)

Creator God, who through the Holy Spirit in the beginning breathed life into the nostrils of humanity, help us to wonder at the miracle of human reproduction, noticing your image imprinted on each person in the family of God, so that we may join together as your children in love and peace and grow your kingdom here on earth. *Amen.*

GIANT MATCHING GAME

Gather around the GIANT WORD poster. Use one of the words from the word bank to fill in each sentence below. Work in small groups. If you don't know the answer, leave it blank or ask someone in your small group to help. If you have a question or need help, raise your hand. The Glossary on page 91 may also help.

1. The period of time when a human (usually a pre-teen or teen) body changes so that sex organs become capable of reproduction is called p_____.

2. Chemicals produced by the endocrine glands, which help regulate body activities are called h_____.

3. Course, curly hair that grows in the genital area of human beings is called p_____ h_____.

4. Cylinder-shaped organ consists of a head or glans (which is the most sensitive part) and a shaft of spongy tissue is called the p_____.

5. Glands that produce hormones and sperm are called t_____.

6. Sudden pushing and squeezing action that forces semen from the penis during orgasm is called e_____.

7. Soft muscle pouch containing and protecting the testicles is called the s_____.

8. Process where blood rushes to the penis causing it to enlarge and stiffen is called an e_____.

9. Operation right after birth where a doctor removes the foreskin of a penis is called c_____.

10. Ejaculation of semen from the penis while sleeping is called n_____ e_____. Another slang term for this is "wet dream."

11. Male reproductive cells manufactured in the testicles and ejaculated in the semen are called s_____.

12. A soft muscular tube about three inches long that makes a passageway from the uterus to the outside of the body is called a v_____.

13. Glands where female reproductive cells are formed and where hormones are reproduces are called o_____.

14. Name for female genitals located between the legs is called the v_____.

15. Hollow organ located inside the female body in the lower abdomen, shaped and sized like an upside-down pear is called the u_____.

16. Small, cylinder shaped organ located just above the urethra made of very sensitive tissue is called the c_____.

17. Organs on the chest that in females produces milk are called b_____.

18. The stage of the female menstrual cycle when the inner lining of the uterus is shed and a small amount of bloody tissue leaves the body through the vagina is called m_____.

19. When a fetus naturally leaves a woman's body before it is time to give birth, the release is called a m_____.

20. A medical procedure to end a pregnancy (usually before the 20th week) is called an a_____.

21. When a baby is born feet or buttocks first, the birth is called b_____.

22. The process of the fetus leaving the female body from the uterus is called l_____.

23. When a male sex cell and a female sex cell join together, the process is called f_____.

24. The tubes that lead from the ovaries to the uterus are called the f_____ t_____.

25. When a fetus is delivered through a surgical procedure that cuts through the tissues of a female abdomen into the uterus it is called a c_____ s_____.

THE MIRACLE OF LIFE

You may have some questions about the video you watched in the session. Write down two or three things that you want to learn more about.

Almighty God, giver of the miracle of life, help us leave this place and enter the world as people who see your grace at work in daily life, going to school, spending time with friends, and being a part of a community. Help us to also see the miracle of our lives, the way we were formed, the way we entered the world, and the way our bodies can make more life. For all of these things we give you thanks, through our Savior, Jesus Christ. *Amen.*

WE ARE CHANGING

Divine Sustainer, who walks with us as we grow from infancy to adulthood, be present with us through all life's changes, those we welcome and those we do not, through the one whose life included both the manger and the cross, our Savior Jesus Christ. *Amen*.

Six days later, Jesus took with him Peter and James and his brother John and led them up a high mountain, by themselves. And he was transfigured before them, and his face shone like the sun, and his clothes became dazzling white. Suddenly there appeared to them Moses and Elijah, talking with him. Then Peter said to Jesus, "Lord, it is good for us to be here; if you wish, I will make three dwellings here, one for you, one for Moses, and one for Elijah." While he was still speaking, suddenly a bright cloud overshadowed them, and from the cloud a voice said, "This is my Son, the Beloved; with him I am well pleased; listen to him!" When the disciples heard this, they fell to the ground and were overcome by fear. But Jesus came and touched them, saying, "Get up and do not be afraid." And when they looked up, they saw no one except Jesus himself alone.

—Matthew 17:1–8

THE TRANSFIGURATION

1. Who are the main characters in the passage?
   a. Jesus, Peter, and John
   b. Jesus, Peter, James, and John
   c. Jesus, Peter, James, John, Moses, Elijah
   d. Jesus, Peter, James, John, Moses, Elijah, "Voice from a cloud"

2. What is the setting of the passage?
   a. A city
   b. A mountain
   c. A dwelling

3. How did Jesus change?
   a. His face shone like the sun and his clothes became dazzling white.
   b. He became angry.
   c. He stopped being friends with the sleepy disciples.

4. How did the story end?
   a. The disciples who were there also started shining bright white.
   b. They built dwelling places at the top of the mountain.
   c. The disciples who were there fell to the ground in fear, and then only Jesus was left.

In our Gospel passage we see that the physical appearance of Jesus changes for just a moment. In this moment, his face shines like the sun and his clothes are dazzling white.

One of the things that Jesus said to his disciples was, "Do not be afraid." Even though we may never experience what the disciples did, we all experience fear. The disciples may have wondered what would happen in the future. They may have wondered how things were going to change. Jesus wants us to remember to not be afraid. We can trust God and remember that God loves us!

What are you afraid of? What worries you?

Thinking about growing up, what are you excited about?

CHANGES

Write down some ways that you have changed in each of the sections below.

CHANGES IN MY		
BODY	MIND	RELATIONSHIPS

Directions: Draw a picture to go with each fill-in-the-blank question. Feel free to add more to statements on the blank space.

Most of my relationships make me feel _____

_____

_____.

I think about _____ all of the time.

A major change I have noticed in my body is _____
_____
_____.

I wonder if the body of Jesus _____
_____
_____.

Dear God, thank you for creating me and helping me to grow and change. Help me to trust in you and to not be afraid. *Amen*.

WE ARE KNOWLEDGEABLE

Holy God, you know how much we need your love. Sometimes we forget that it is always here waiting for us to accept can separate us from your love. As we spend time learning and becoming more knowledgeable, remind us of your unconditional love for us. *Amen*.

"As for me, this is my covenant with you:
You shall be the ancestor of a multitude of nations.
No longer shall your name be Abram,
but your name shall be Abraham;
for I have made you the ancestor of a multitude of nations.
I will make you exceedingly fruitful;
and I will make nations of you,
and kings shall come from you.
I will establish my covenant between me and you,
and your offspring after you throughout their generations,
for an everlasting covenant,
to be God to you and to your offspring after you.
—Genesis 17:4–7

SEXUALITY SQUABBLE GAME

There are six different topics discussed on these pages that will give you the answers you need for the game we are about to play. The topics are: STIs, HIV/AIDS, dating and falling in love, technology safety, sexuality, and sexual abuse.

Use the space below to write notes or questions you may have as we play this game.

HIV/AIDS

AIDS stands for Acquired Immunodeficiency Syndrome. It is the late stage of an infection caused by a virus that can be transmitted from an infected person to an uninfected person by an exchange of blood, breast milk, semen, vaginal mucus, urine, or feces. HIV stands for human immunodeficiency virus. HIV is a type of STI—sexually transmitted infection. It is the virus that can lead to AIDS, if left untreated. You may hear the disease called HIV/AIDS. HIV attacks the immune system of the body—the system that fights off disease. The virus prevents the immune system from doing its job properly, so the body is unable to defend against diseases that it may usually fight—pneumonia, for example—and some rare diseases that people with healthy immune systems seldom have because their healthy immune systems prevent illness.

Many teenagers believe that they don't have to be worried about HIV because they aren't gay or they don't use drugs. However, we should remember that if a person has sex, he or she may be exposed to the infection from their sexual partner. People can be infected with HIV if they participate in behaviors that place them at risk. These behaviors include the following:

1. Having sexual contact with an infected person

2. The sharing of needles and syringes by users of drugs

3. Unsafe ear piercing and tattooing

4. Being infected (as a mother) and passing the infection a baby before or during birth

5. Having an unsafe blood transfusion (People have received transfusions of blood from donors who were infected with HIV and have become infected. However, the procedures that are now used to test blood donations have made blood transfusions in the United States very safe.)

HIV may be found in blood, semen, and vaginal fluids. The virus may enter the body of anyone coming into contact with infected fluids through sexual contact, sharing of needles, and unsafe piercing and tattooing. HIV/AIDS is not spread through casual contact. Casual contact with a person who has AIDS is not a threat to you. Using a public toilet, drinking from a fountain, and playing sports with or eating with an infected person doesn't endanger you.

Because the symptoms of HIV may not appear until long after a person has been infected, it is not always possible to tell whether or not a person has HIV. Therefore, the only way to be completely safe is to avoid behaviors that may put you at risk for HIV.

STIs

Sexually transmitted infections, or STIs, are passed from one person to another through sexual contact. There are more than twenty different STIs. Some of the diseases you might hear about are syphilis, gonorrhea, chlamydia, and genital herpes. Some STIs can be treated and cured. Others are not curable, meaning that people will have the disease for life and continue to be able to pass it along to others.

The symptoms commonly associated with STIs include the following:

- Unusual discharge (leaking of thick fluid) from the penis or vagina

- Irritation, lumps, or sores on or around the genitals

- Pain or tenderness in the genitals, genital area, or abdomen

- Painful urination or frequent need to urinate

These symptoms do not automatically mean that a person has a STI. In fact, a person can have an STI and have no symptoms. These symptoms can also indicate the presence of other diseases—diseases that are not sexually transmitted. However, people who are sexually active and have any of these symptoms are advised to see their doctor.

You can get an STI from sexual contact. In order to pass an STI from one body to another, there must be direct contact with the viruses or bacteria that cause the STI. This kind of contact generally happens during sexual activity. The viruses and bacteria that cause STIs are often found in bodily fluids.

They are also found in places in the body that are warm and moist, such as those found in places like the penis, vulva, vagina, rectum, mouth, or throat. By touching those places on another person who has an STI, one may be infected. It is unusual for STIs to spread in ways other than human-to-human contact, like on a toilet seat.

Responsible sexual behavior is the best prevention for STIs. For young people, responsible sexual behavior means waiting until they are much older to become sexually active.

Dating and Falling in Love

Dating is one way young people get to know each other. Dating is in many ways like other acts of friendship. You talk, laugh, and do things together. Friendships generally start with things that people have in common: living near each other, enjoying the same activities, or sitting beside each other in class.

Friends who are dating have things in common too; the fact that they are attracted to each other adds a special element. People are drawn together because they are alike in many ways and because they are different.

When you begin to date you should learn to understand yourself, your feelings, and the way your mind and body reacts when you are close to another person. Talk together about your feelings. Your ability to communicate is a sign of your maturity and readiness for dating.

Be true to yourself. Show respect for yourself and for each other. God gave us gifts to share that are meant to uplift each other. Being with someone you love should make you want to be a better person, not a different person!

We were created by God to love many people, not just one. Many of the people we meet will be possible life-long partners for us, not just one. You will be meeting lots of people in the next several years. You will be developing friendships with some of the people you meet. You may want to build deeper friendships with some of those friends and eventually work at building relationships and intimacy. Perhaps there will be one special person you will decide to marry.

What questions should I ask myself to discern if I am in love?

- With whom do I enjoy spending time more than anyone else?

- Who makes me feel good about myself?

- Who do I enjoy discovering new things about?

- Who values the things I consider to be important?

- Who wants to be close to me but doesn't insist that we do everything together?

- Can I trust this person with my personal thoughts and feelings?

Infatuation is an immature, unreasonable love that is common among young people who are still new at relationships and who are searching for their own identity. Many young people confuse feelings of love with feelings of infatuation. There is nothing wrong with infatuation—it can be very exciting. But it is important not to let feelings of infatuation trick you into behaviors or commitments that really belong in mature love relationships.

When you are in love, you tend to be more loving toward others and may feel like you are becoming the best person you can become through Christ's love for you. Love inspires a person to be the best they can be!

Technology Safety

Technology has given us many new ways of communicating and staying in touch with people all over the world. With this great tool, there are things we always need to keep in mind:

- Bullying via the internet, cell phone, or Facebook is still bullying. What you type is permanent. You can't take it back.

- Bullying won't help you make or keep the kind of friends that will be good friends to you.

- Anything put on the internet is public and permanent.

- Texting, email, and networking sites are not truly private or anonymous.

- People on the internet can hide their real identity.

There are many ways to use technology responsibly:

- Use the grandmother test: Don't post anything online that you wouldn't want your grandmother to see.

- Nothing is private! Assume anything you send or post may be sent to other people.

- Hurtful words are wrong whether you say them or type them.

- Don't give in to the pressure to do something that makes you uncomfortable, even online.

- No regrets. Think about the feelings of other people before you text or email something that maybe unkind. You will regret hurting others.

Pornography is often found on the internet. Pornography is any image that exploits sexuality and misuses the gift of sexuality. Any picture or image that that turns people into sex objects, promotes sexual relations between children and adults, or links sex and violence together is pornography.

Anytime you see sexuality being exploited, or used as a way to make money, you are probably looking at pornography. Pornography is addictive, so it is easy to sell once a person's normal curiosity gets "hooked." If you see pictures or get onto a website that you know shows pornography, tell your parents immediately.

Sexual Abuse

Much attention has been given to the subject of sexual abuse. We are beginning to recognize that the problem is widespread. We have been telling children to be careful of strangers, but we haven't told them why. We're trying to do a better job of informing young people about the dangers of sexual abuse in hopes that greater awareness will decrease the problems.

To abuse something is to use it in an improper or destructive way. Sex abusers use sex in an improper and destructive way. Most often people who are abusive are misusing their power to hurt someone else. They also may have been abused themselves as children and be confused about the place of sex in their lives. In most cases, sex abusers are acquaintances— even friends and relatives. Most sex abusers are men, but women can be abusive as well. Because it is against the law to abuse a person sexually, sex abusers are guilty of a sexual crime.

You are in control of your body. Anytime anyone touches you or asks you to do things related to sex that make you feel uncomfortable, tell them to stop and share your feelings with a trustworthy adult. Your friends should do the same thing, if they find themselves in this situation.

What are some new things that you learned?

What are some things that you want to learn more about?

ABRAHAM AND SARAH

When Abram was ninety-nine years old, the Lord appeared to Abram, and said to him, "I am God Almighty; walk before me, and be blameless. And I will make my covenant between me and you, and will make you exceedingly numerous." Then Abram fell on his face; and God said to him, "As for me, this is my covenant with you: You shall be the ancestor of a multitude of nations. No longer shall your name be Abram, but your name shall be Abraham; for I have made you the ancestor of a multitude of nations. I will make you exceedingly fruitful; and I will make nations of you, and kings shall come from you. I will establish my covenant between me and you, and your offspring after you throughout their generations, for an everlasting covenant, to be God to you and to your offspring after you.

God said to Abraham, "As for Sarai your wife, you shall not call her Sarai, but Sarah shall be her name. I will bless her, and moreover I will give you a son by her. I will bless her, and she shall give rise to nations; kings of peoples shall come from her." Then Abraham fell on his face and laughed, and said to himself, "Can a child be born to a man who is a hundred years old? Can Sarah, who is ninety years old, bear a child?" And Abraham said to God, "O that Ishmael might live in your sight!" God said, "No, but your wife Sarah shall bear you a son, and you shall name him Isaac. I will establish my covenant with him as an everlasting covenant for his offspring after him. As for Ishmael, I have heard you; I will bless him and make him fruitful and exceedingly numerous; he shall be the father of twelve princes, and I will make him a great nation. But my covenant I will establish with Isaac, whom Sarah shall bear to you at this season next year." And when he had finished talking with him, God went up from Abraham.

—Genesis 17:1–7, 15–22

WE ARE COMPLEX

Love is patient; love is kind;
love is not envious or boastful
or arrogant or rude.
It does not insist on its own way;
it is not irritable or resentful;
it does not rejoice in wrongdoing,
but rejoices in the truth.
It bears all things, believes all things,
hopes all things, endures all things.
—1 Corinthians 13: 4–7

Most Holy God, who invites us to live as people of love and grace, help us to see you at work as we seek to understand how we are each unique. *Amen*.

GENDER

Gender is a word we use to talk about others and ourselves. Gender is felt inside of ourselves and expressed to others. When we show or express to others our gender, we call that gender expression. When we feel or sense our gender in our minds and hearts, we call that gender identity.

Sometimes, people think gender is the same as biological sex, or whether a person is male, female, or a born with both male and female organs. Gender is separate.

Say we were to draw an arc, like this. At one end we might put feminine. At the other end we might put masculine. In between are endless other points.

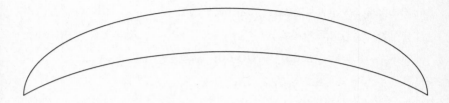

On this arc we could put the statements that we just used in the game we played.

Understanding who we are, both inside and out, is a life long journey. At this point in life, it is OK not to know everything about yourself yet. You may want to take this home and think about how you express gender to others.

"I" Quiz:

1. When I get dressed in the morning, I usually think about . . .
   a. my overall look.
   b. whether I will stand out.
   c. if I have a "cool" outfit on.
   d. only what I want and just grab something.
   e. All of the above

2. I like to mainly wear the color . . .
   a. red.
   b. blue.
   c. black.
   d. pink.
   e. None of the above

3. Even though my classmates sometimes _____, I don't feel comfortable doing it.
   a. wear makeup
   b. play sports
   c. wear skirts
   d. grow their hair long
   e. _____ (Make up your own response.)

4. When I think about how I feel, I would say . . .
    a. I feel mostly like a girl.
    b. I feel mostly like a boy.
    c. I don't know how I feel about my gender.

5. I feel like my body_____.

(You will find some explanations about each of these questions on page 85.)

God, help us feel your love. When we feel lonely or afraid, help us find strength to be brave. Help us to share our fears and hopes with others. *Amen*.

WE ARE
MATURING

And Jesus increased in wisdom and in years
and in divine human favor.
—Luke 2:52

THE BOY JESUS IN THE TEMPLE

Now every year his parents went to Jerusalem for the festival of the Passover. And when he was twelve years old, they went up as usual for the festival. When the festival was ended and they started to return, the boy Jesus stayed behind in Jerusalem, but his parents did not know it. Assuming that he was in the group of travelers, they went a day's journey. Then they started to look for him among their relatives and friends.

When they did not find him, they returned to Jerusalem to search for him. After three days they found him in the temple, sitting among the teachers, listening to them and asking them questions. And all who heard him were amazed at his understanding and his answers. When his parents saw him they were astonished; and his mother said to him, "Child, why have you treated us like this? Look, your father and I have been searching for you in great anxiety." He said to them, "Why were you searching for me? Did you not know that I must be in my Father's house?" But they did not understand what he said to them. Then he went down with them and came to Nazareth, and was obedient to them. His mother treasured all these things in her heart.

And Jesus increased in wisdom and in years, and in divine and human favor.

—Luke 2:41–52

What must have been difficult for Jesus' parents?

How might Jesus have felt in the temple learning from and teaching the priests and scribes?

How do children and teens grow in "increased in wisdom and in years, and in divine and human favor"? What might that mean today?

How have you increased in wisdom and in years, and how have you increased in divine and human favor?

What surprised you?

What did you see in a new or fresh way?

PARENT INTERVIEW

Ask your parent the following questions beginning with the phrase: When you were my age . . .

- What was your favorite TV show?

- What kind of music did you listen to?

- How did you feel about your parent's type of music?

- Did you have a best friend?

- What did you like doing?

- What did you want to become when you grew up?

- What household rule did you like least when you were growing up?

- Did you have your own telephone?

- Did you have a good relationship with your parents?

- Could you talk to your parents about anything?

- What was the greatest pressure you experienced when you were my age?

- What did you learn about your parents?

Jesus said, "You are the light of the world. A city built on a hill cannot be hid. No one lights a lamp to put it under a bucket, but on a lamp-stand where it gives light for everyone in the house. And you, like the lamp, must shed light among your fellow men, so that they may see the good you do, and give glory to your Father in heaven."

—Matthew 5:14–16

Dear gracious and loving God, who knows the joy of tweens, parents and family. Our hearts are full of gratitude for these parent and tweens here today. We thank you for the gifts that you have given them and the light that they bring into the world through your grace. Help them to fill their homes with the light of your love and keep them ever closer to each other and to you. In your Son's name we pray. *Amen*.

"I" QUIZ EXPLANATION

When I get dressed in the morning, I usually think about . . .

No matter what you decide to wear, you are a child of God! Clothes can be an expression of how we feel about ourselves. Try to avoid falling into the trap of our culture that says how you look is who you are. You are so much more than your clothes, hair, and physical appearance. Sometimes, we use clothes to express our gender to others, and that is OK. Have you ever thought about that before? Record some of your thoughts about why you dress the way you do. Consider sharing them with your parents.

I like to mainly wear the color . . .

Can colors really be assigned to one group of people? Aren't colors a "neutral" category? Think about why you wear a certain color most of the time. Is it because you like that color? Is it because it is a favorite sports team's color? Do you even get to choose, or is it whatever your parents buy you? The key to expressing yourself is feeling free to be YOU, fully you! If wearing a color that many people think is only for "girls" or only for "boys" makes you feel more like yourself, consider talking to your parents about it.

Write about your thoughts here.

Even though my classmates sometimes _____

_____*,*

I don't feel comfortable doing it.

The choices on this list are often associated with one group of people. Ask yourself, why don't I feel comfortable wearing makeup? Why don't I feel comfortable playing sports? Why don't I feel comfortable wearing skirts? Why don't I feel comfortable growing my hair long? Does it have anything to do with how you express your gender? Write about your thoughts here.

When I think about how I feel, I would say . . .

Gender identity is the way you feel about yourself. If you have questions about this, talk to your parents. Talk to a leader in your church or the facilitator of this program. Write your thoughts about it here.

I feel like my body_____.

Consider writing as many possible answers to this fill in the blank as you can. Try to think of at least five, but maybe even ten. Then, share those with your parents.

GLOSSARY

abortion. The termination and expulsion of a pregnancy before birth.

abstinence. A decision to not do what a person wants to do; also called celibacy or "saying no"; sexual abstinence is choosing not to engage in sexual activity.

abuse. To abuse something is to use it in an improper or destructive way.

adolescence. The period in human growth and development that occurs after childhood and before adulthood, from ages 10 to 19. This is a rapid and significant period of human development.

aggressive behavior. An unhealthy way of getting your way by attacking others; forceful or violent acts; can include yelling, screaming, hitting, biting, kicking, slamming doors, and pushing. More serious forms of aggression that are illegal include rape, physical attack, assault, and shooting.

AIDS. Abbreviation for acquired immunodeficiency syndrome; a disease caused by a virus that can be transmitted from an infected person to an uninfected person only by an exchange of blood, semen, vaginal mucus, urine, or feces; type of sexually transmitted infection.

assertive behavior. A healthy, positive way of expressing your own needs.

assigned sex. Sex assigned at birth.

attraction. When someone is physically drawn to another person or sees someone as desirable.

biological sex. The physical body parts, genetic make-up, and hormones of an individual's body; refers to the physical body parts of an individual's body at birth.

body image. The way you see yourself, imagine how you look, and feel about your body.

condoms. A sheath worn over the penis to catch the semen during ejaculation; a form of birth control; can reduce the risk of contracting HIV/AIDS.

cyber bullying. Bullying and aggressive behavior using technology like texting, e-mailing, and posting to share offensive or hurtful pictures or comments about other people.

circumcision. An operation during which a doctor removes the foreskin of the penis.

clitoris. Small, cylinder-shaped organ located just above the urethra made of very sensitive tissue.

ejaculation. Sudden pushing and squeezing action that forces semen from the penis during male orgasm.

erection. Process by which the blood rushes into the penis causing it to enlarge and stiffen.

flirting. A playful behavior intended to arouse sexual interest or to make playfully romantic or sexual overtures.

friendship. The connecting bond of affection between people. Friendship includes loyalty, respect, mutuality, and commitment.

gay. A person who is attracted to a person of the same sex often calls him or herself *gay* or *homosexual*.

gender. A socially determined way of describing human beings based on characteristics like appearance, dress, reproductive organs, and behavior, now thought of as a continuum or spectrum.

gender expression. The way a person interprets their gender with outward displays of that gender stereotype.

gender identity. Built upon what an individual senses internally about their own gender.

gender roles. Society's set of roles, values, and expectations for what it means to be a girl/woman or a boy/man in a particular culture. Gender roles vary from culture to culture and over time.

genetic makeup. Refers to whether scientific tests determine a person has xx, xy, or another makeup of chromosomes.

heterosexuality. People who are attracted to people of opposite genders often call themselves *heterosexual* or *straight*.

HIV. Human immunodeficiency virus; the virus that leads to AIDS; commonly referred to as HIV/AIDS.

homosexuality. Romantic attraction, sexual attraction, or sexual behavior between members of the same sex or gender. A woman who is attracted to other women often calls herself *gay*, *lesbian*, or *homosexual*. A man who is attracted to other men often calls himself *gay* or *homosexual*.

hormones. Testosterone, progesterone, and estrogen are hormones connected to human sexuality.

Imago Dei. "Image of God," denoting the symbolic relation between God and humanity.

inclusive language. Language that seeks to include all people, rather than only a few.

infatuation. Immature and fleeting attraction between people.

knowledge. General understanding or familiarity with a principle or term gained through experience or learning.

lesbian. A woman who is attracted to other women.

LGBTQ+. The acronym for *Lesbian, Gay, Bisexual, Transgender, Queer, Questioning, Intersex, Asexual, Ally*. An inclusive term that seeks to capture all sexual and gender identities other than heterosexual. This is an evolving term, as our understanding and language around sexuality expands and matures.

love. A mature love includes acceptance, non-judgment, and a commitment to help another person grow emotionally and spiritually; respects the dignity of another person; a deep, tender, ineffable feeling of affection toward a person. Love arises in families, in friendships, and through a sense of underlying oneness.

masturbation. Touching, rubbing, or stimulating one's own sex organs, producing a pleasurable feeling and sexual excitement.

menstruation. Stage of female menstrual cycle when the inner lining of the uterus is shed and a small amount of bloody tissue leaves the body through the vagina.

miscarriage. The sudden ending of a pregnancy by the body.

nocturnal emission. Ejaculation of semen from the penis while male is sleeping. Another name for this is *wet dream*. Only about a teaspoon of semen is released from the penis during ejaculation.

orgasm. The pleasurable and intense release of tension built up as sexual excitement.

ovaries. Glands where female reproductive cells are formed and where hormones are produced. The ovaries release an egg each month that travels down the fallopian tubes toward the uterus.

penis. Cylinder-shaped organ that consist of a head or glands (which is the most sensitive part) and a shaft of soft spongy tissue.

petting. Any touching of sex organs other than intercourse.

physical anatomy. The structure of the human body. This includes terms relevant to sexuality like penis, ovaries, vagina, and testicles.

pornography. Any image that exploits sexuality and misuses the gift of sexuality.

prostitute. A person—woman, man, girl, boy—who is paid to perform sexual acts.

puberty. Time in a young person's life when the body goes from being a child's body to an adult's body. The body becomes able to reproduce. The period of time when pre-teens' and teenagers' bodies change and when the sex organs become capable of reproduction.

pubic hair. Coarse, curly hair that grows in the genital area.

questioning. To be unsure or less certain of your sexual orientation. You can also question your gender identity. People figure out their sexuality and gender identity at different points in their lives, and there's no wrong way to identify.

rape. To force another person to submit to sex acts is a crime, called *rape*.

refusal skills. The ability and learned techniques to assertively say "no" to sexual advances.

romantic attraction. Attraction that makes people desire romantic contact or interaction with another person or persons.

scrotum. Soft muscle pouch containing and protecting the testicles.

sexuality. A great gift from God; ". . . a central aspect of being human throughout life encompasses sex, gender identities and roles, sexual orientation, eroticism, pleasure, intimacy, and reproduction. Sexuality is experienced and expressed in thoughts, fantasies, desires, beliefs, attitudes, values, behaviors, practices, roles, and relationships. While sexuality can include all of these dimensions, not all of them are always experienced or expressed. Sexuality is influenced by the interaction of biological, psychological, social, economic, political, cultural, legal, historical, religious, and spiritual factors."[3]

sexual attraction. Attraction that makes people desire sexual contact or show sexual interest in another person.

---

3   WHO, 2006a www.who.int/topics/sexual_health/en/.

sexual harassment. A feeling of intense annoyance caused by being tormented. This tormenting is caused by continued unwanted contact and attention or persistent attacks and criticism.

sexual intercourse. Sexual activity between two people, especially penetration of the vagina, anus, or mouth.

sexual orientation. A person's emotional, romantic, and sexual attraction to individuals of a particular gender (male or female). Sexual orientation involves a person's feelings and sense of identity; it may or may not be evident in the person's appearance or behavior. People may have attractions to people of the same or opposite sex, but they may elect not to act on these feelings.

sperm. Male reproductive cells manufactured by the testicles and ejaculated in the semen. These cells enter the female egg and begin the fertilization process.

temptation. The desire to have or do something you know you should avoid.

testicles. In males, these are the glands that produce hormones and sperm.

transgender. The "T" in LGBTQ+. Some people have a gender identity that does not match up with their biological sex. For example, they were born with "female" sex organs (vulva, vagina, uterus), but they feel like a male. People in this community sometimes call themselves *transgender* or *trans*. Trans can also include people who do not identify with the strict male/female gender roles the world tells us we should fit into. Sometimes people who do not feel either male or female call themselves *genderqueer*. (*Note:* Terms like *transgendered*, *tranny*, or *he-she* are old-fashioned and hurtful.)

uterus. Hollow organ located inside the women's body in the lower abdomen, shaped and sized like an upside-down pear.

vagina. A soft muscular tube about 3 inches long that makes a passageway from the uterus to the outside of the body; this opening is very stretchy and expands to become the birth canal when a baby is born.

virgin. A person who has never had sexual intercourse. This term can be applied to both males and females.

vulnerability. Emotionally opening ourselves up to other people.

vulva. Name for the female genitals located between the legs; this name is the general name for the entire female genital area.

womb. Refers to the uterus; the reference is often found in the Bible.

PRAYERS

The Lord's Prayer

Our Father, who are in heaven,
  hallowed be thy Name,
  thy kingdom come,
  thy will be done,
    on earth as it is in heaven.
Give us this day our daily bread.
And forgive us our trespasses,
  as we forgive those
    who trespass against us.
And lead us not into temptation,
  but deliver us from evil.
For thine is the kingdom,
  and the power, and the glory,
  for ever and ever. *Amen.*

Accepting Myself[4]

God of all people and all creation,
You made me. You know me.
You love each and every part of me:
every cell, every organ, every single hair.
I am beautiful in your sight.
Hold me fast when others do not accept me,
Fill me with your love when I do not accept myself.
Strengthen my spirit.
Fill my heart with celebration.
Endure with me until that time when
others see that I am beautiful,
others accept me for who I am.
All of me.

....

4   Sharon Ely Pearson and Jenifer C. Gamber, *Call on Me: A Prayer Book for Young People* (New York: Morehouse, 2012), 58.

Feeling Close to God[5]

I feel the sunshine on my face
    and the warmth of your love that surrounds me.
The beating of my heart and the expansion of my lungs
    remind me of the life within me.
With you, God, I live and move, and have my being.

In the stillness of my being and the movement of my
    body, I am amazed at how alive I am.
My thoughts and memories connect my past and my
    present, as I anticipate the future.
With you, God, I live, and move, and have my being.

Your hand is always on my shoulder.
With you, God, I live, and move, and have my being.

5   *Call on Me*, 30.

Body Image[6]

Creator God, you made all things.
You made us in your image and blessed us.

Help me to see that you bless me too.
Bless my hand and foot,
    finger and toe,
    chest and head,
    eyes and hair,
    height and weight.
You made every part of me
    and I am beautiful.

Help me turn away from things and people
    that tell me I'm ugly,
    that I don't fit in.

I am awesome and wonderfully made.
Help me believe this.

....

6   *Call on Me*, 61.